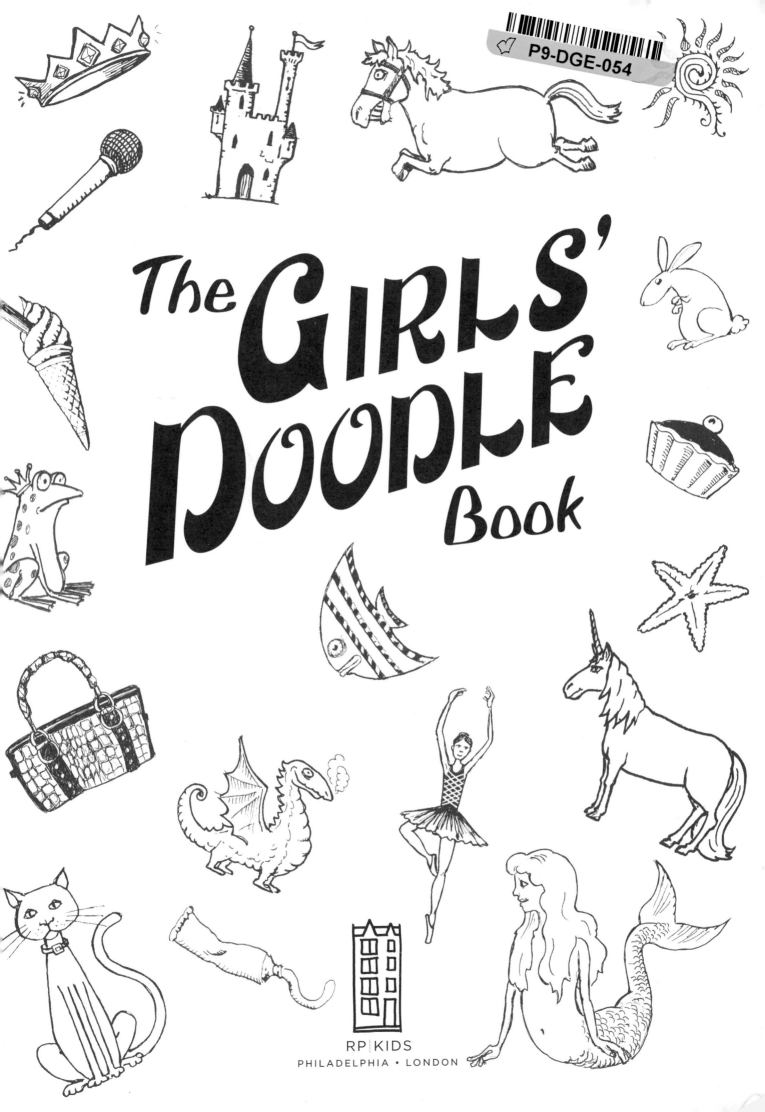

The GIRLS' DOODLE Book

RP|KIDS
PHILADELPHIA • LONDON

Copyright © 2008 Buster Books

All rights reserved under the Pan-American
and International Copyright Conventions

First published in Great Britain by Buster Books,
an imprint of Michael O'Mara Books Limited, 2008

First published in the United States
by Running Press Book Publishers, 2008

Printed in the United States

15   14   13   12   11
Digit on the right indicates the number of this printing

ISBN 978-0-7624-3505-0

Illustrated by Andrew Pinder

This edition published by Running Press Kids,
an imprint of
Running Press Book Publishers
2300 Chestnut Street
Philadelphia, PA 19103-4371

Visit us on the web!
www.runningpress.com

Draw the best bouquet.

Give the fish a fabulous home.

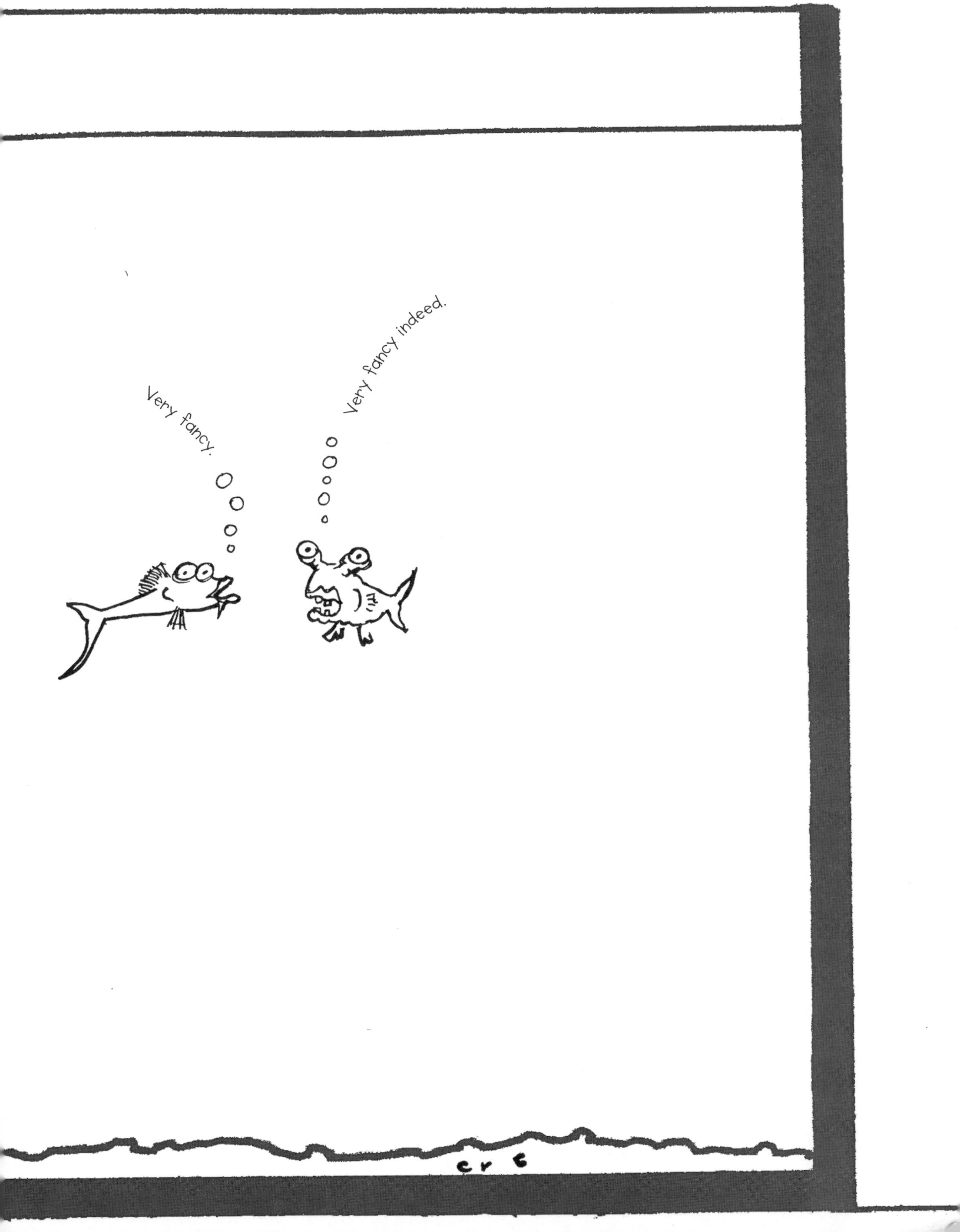
Very fancy.
Very fancy indeed.

Populate the penguin colony.

Will I grow up to be like you?

I am a Gucci Poochi.

Fill the hamsters' cage with fun.

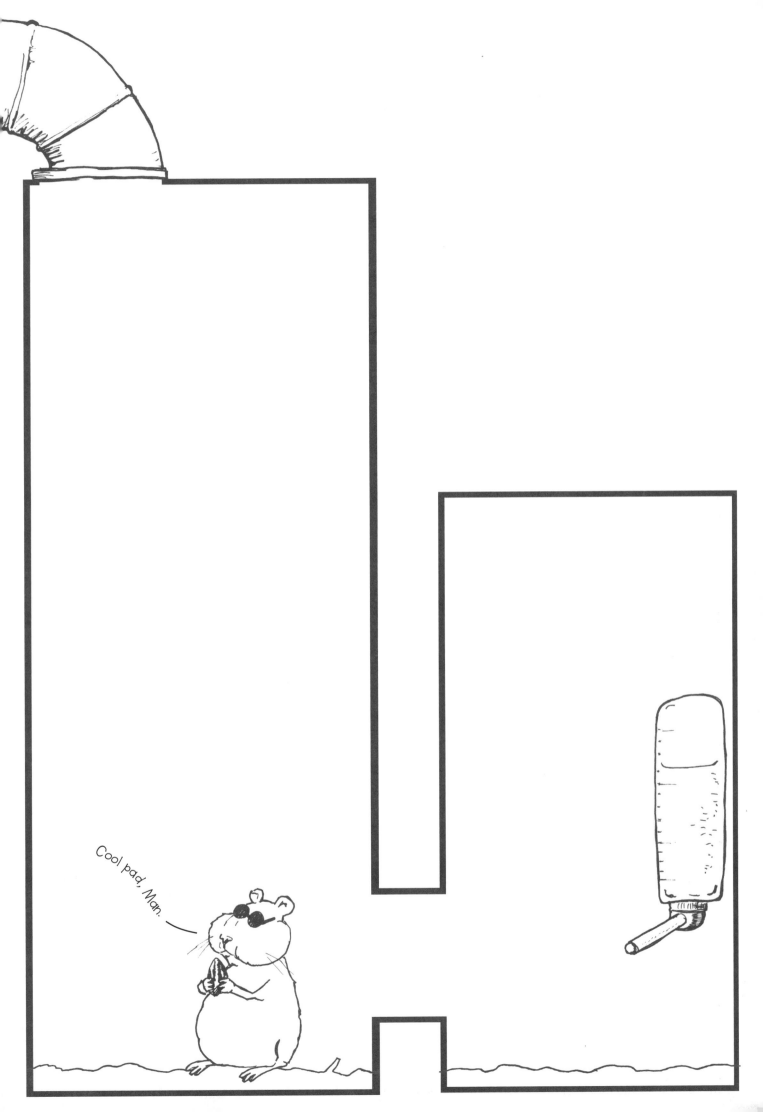

Give Mademoiselle big hair.

Add a pal for the parrot.

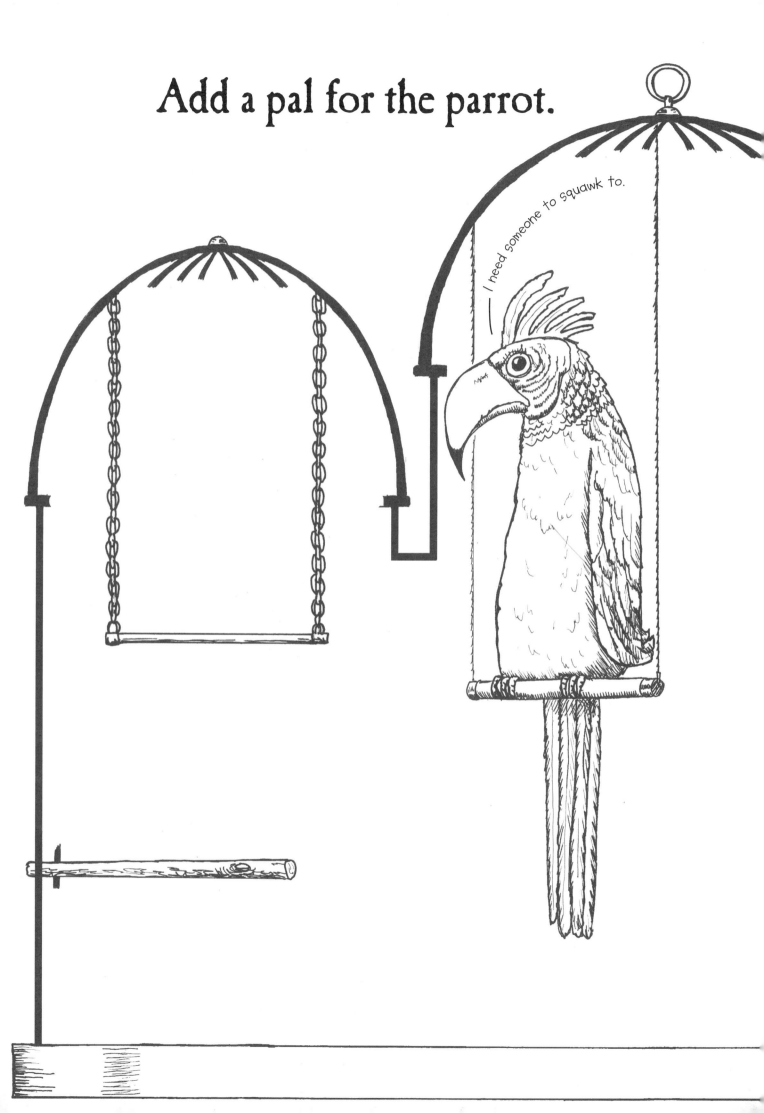

Where are the fairies hiding?

What is Coco juggling?

Oh, no! What has Gran knitted now?

Fill the pond with lilies.

Decorate her hands with henna.

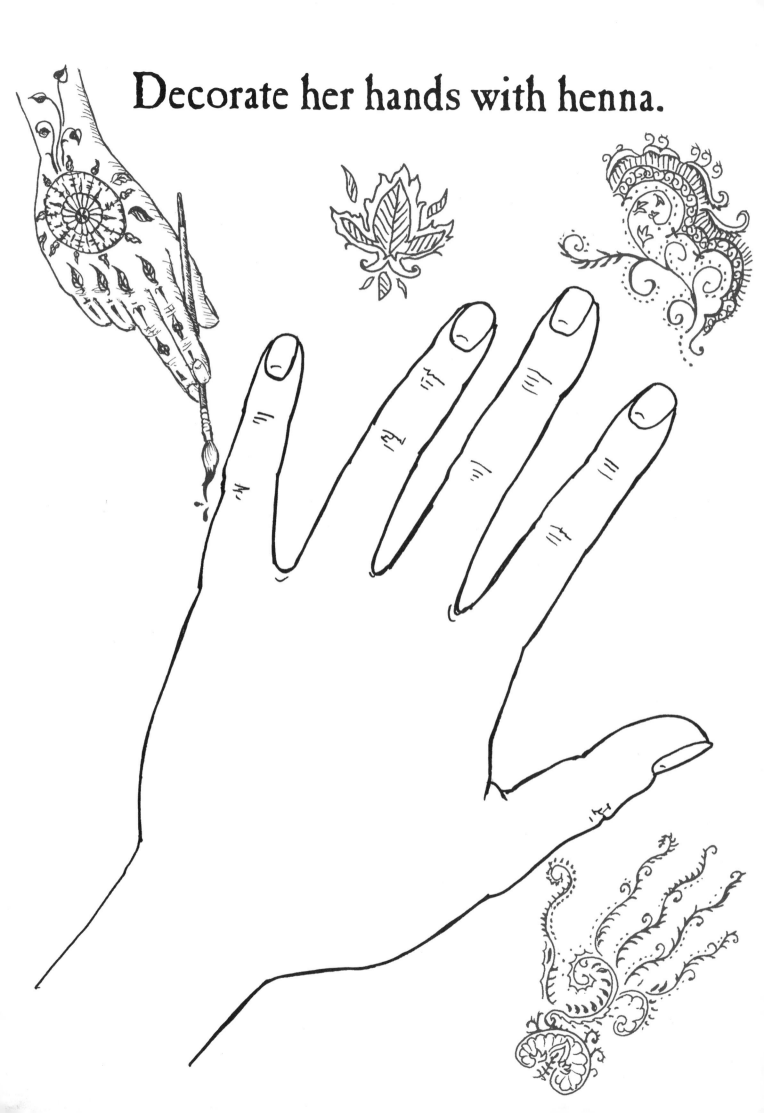

Shower the diva with flowers.

Imagine a mermaid's treasure.

It's mine, all mine.

Design the world's coolest phone.

My phone's got wi-fi, bluetooth, MP3, GPS, video, a camera, SMS. It's hands-free and bakes cakes.

What has she built on the beach?

Who is in the burrow?

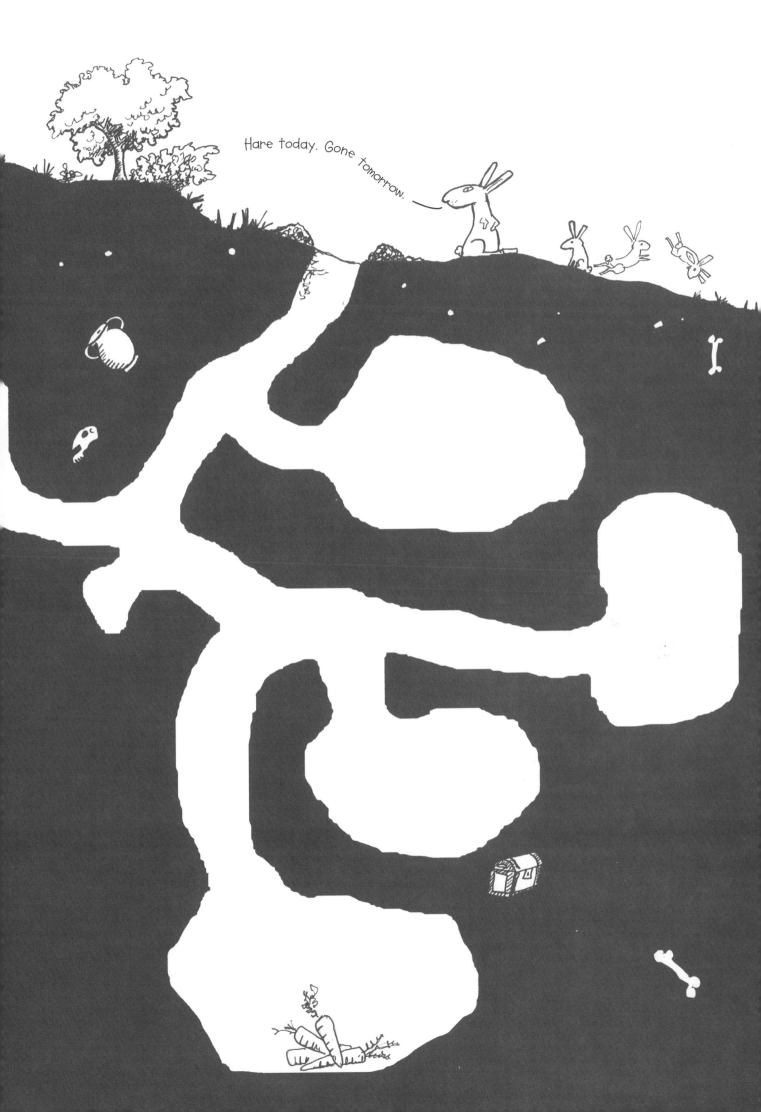

What are the dogs chasing?

Say cheese!

Draw the world's biggest
and rarest butterfly.

Draw Bo Peep's sheep.

Don't tell me you lost them again!

Draw a leaping dolphin.

Show-off.

Decorate the box with shells.

Paint their faces,
fans, and kimonos.

What is in her magic potion?

What will the frog turn into?

Who laid these eggs?

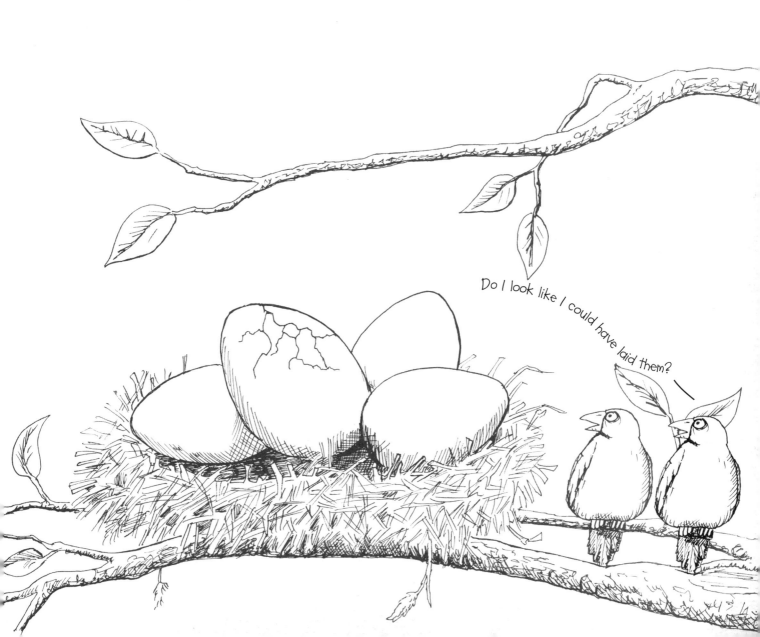

Do I look like I could have laid them?

Finish building these igloos.

Picture a beach paradise.

Aloha!

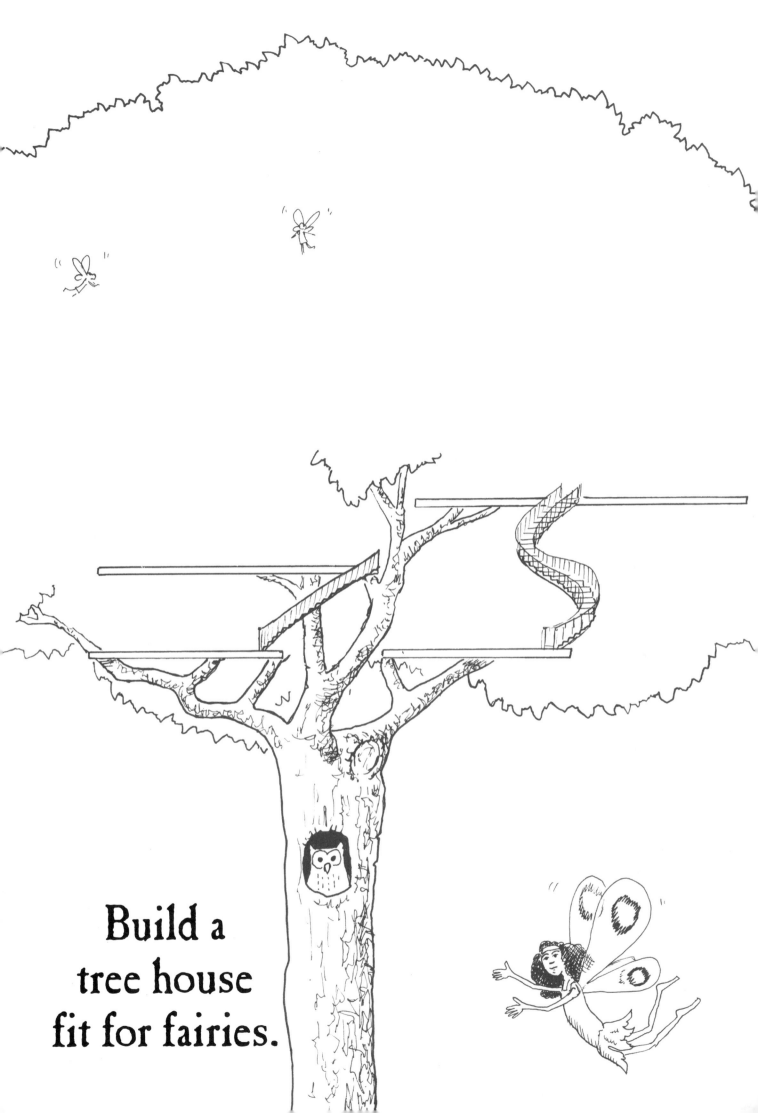

Build a
tree house
fit for fairies.

Can you finish the maze?

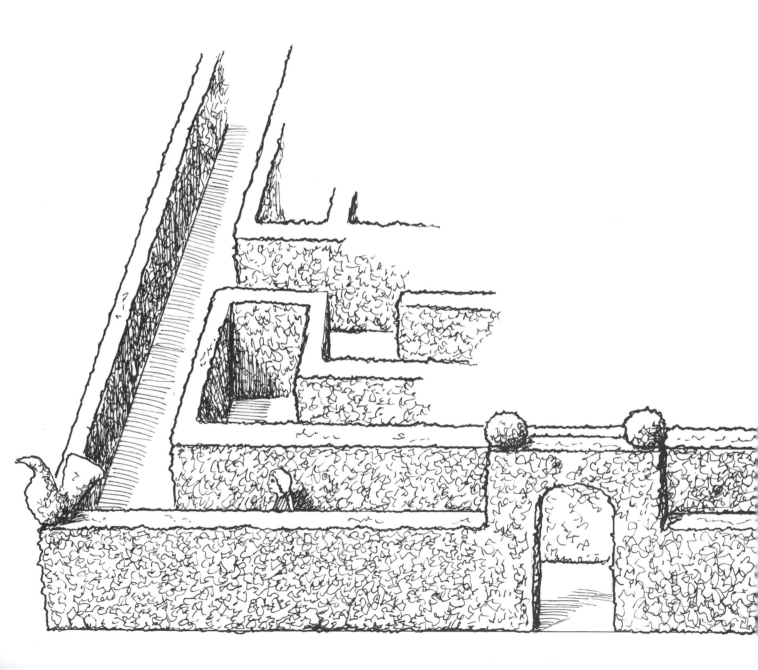

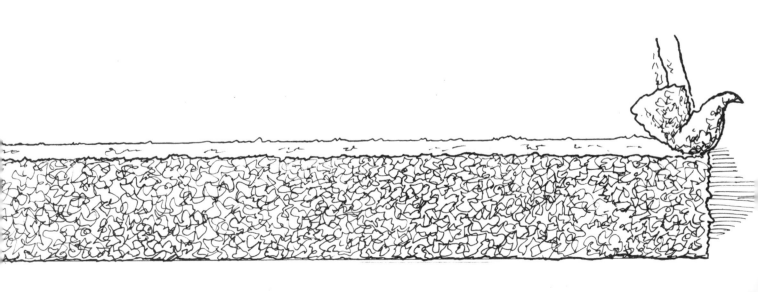

Decorate their tepees.

What would you take to a desert island?

Welcome to Tortoise Island.

Finish the slide.

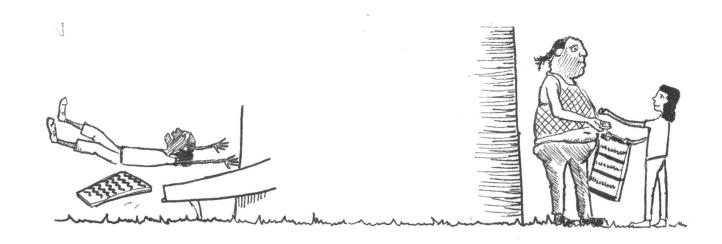

The smaller the better.

Draw some
miniature masterpieces.

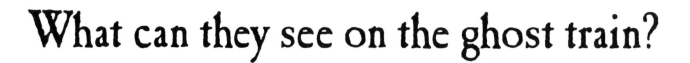

What can they see on the ghost train?

SPOOKY!

Decorate their saris . . .

. . . but don't forget the elephant's coat.

When it is complete make a wish.

Finish the daisy chain.

Design the world's most valuable tiara.

Make the sunflowers grow.

Complete this comic strip.

Put a tail on the bird of paradise.

I think that would really suit me.

What can they see in this Winter Wonderland?

Who is climbing the mountain?

What is on at the movies?

Shhhhh!

Who is driving the car?

What is in the secret garden?

A feast fit for a king.

Draw the kittens in the shop.

How many butterflies?

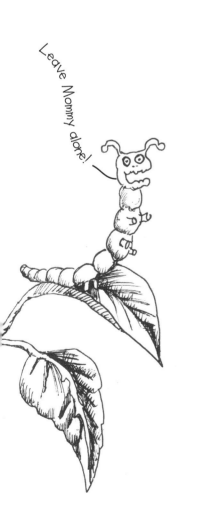

Where is she landing?

Twirl her ribbon.

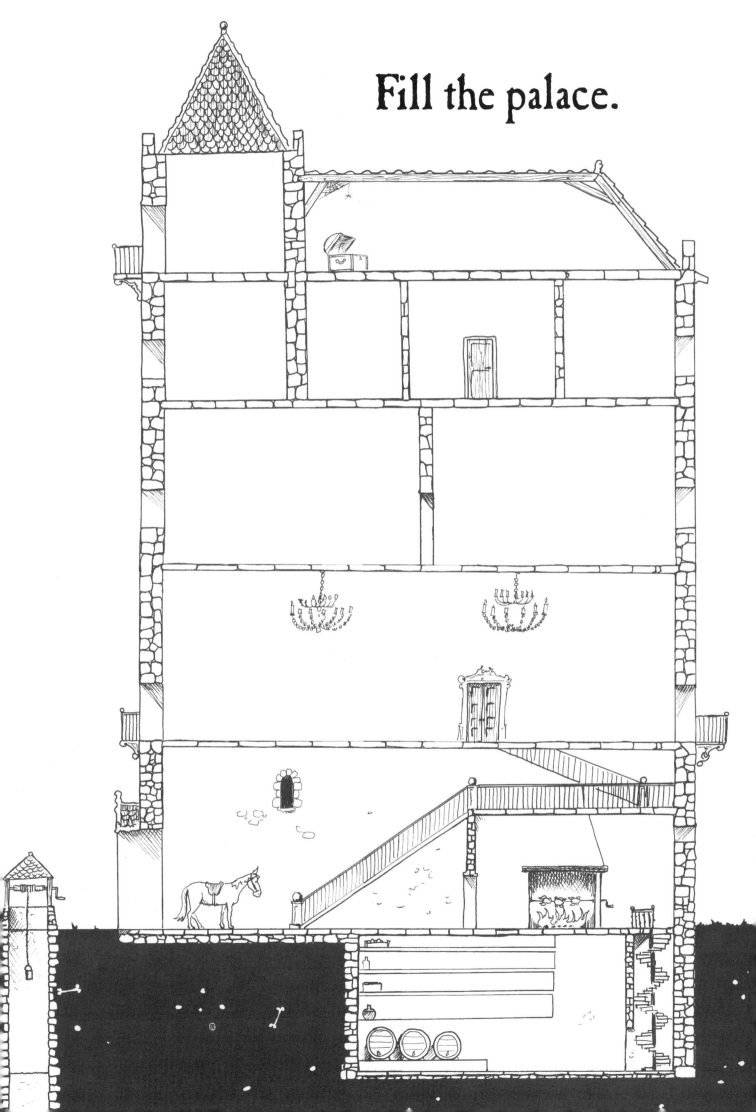

Fill the palace.

What is below the balloon?

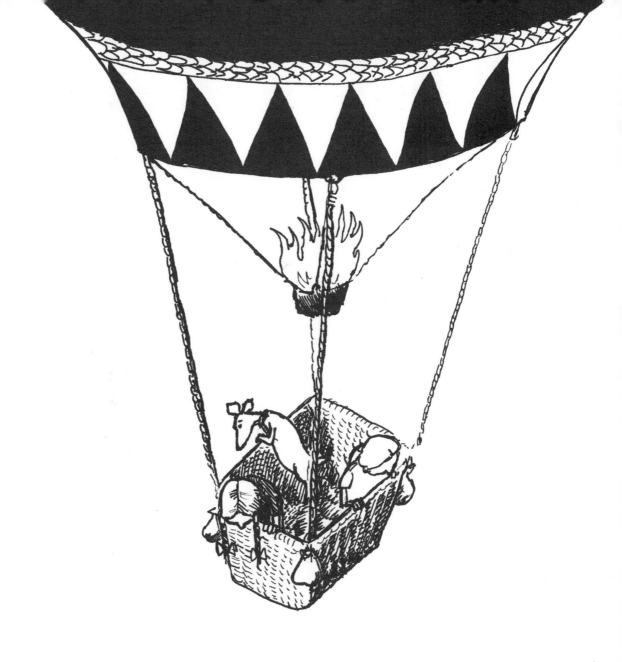

Yummy!

Who is sailing the yacht?

Show a spectacular dive.

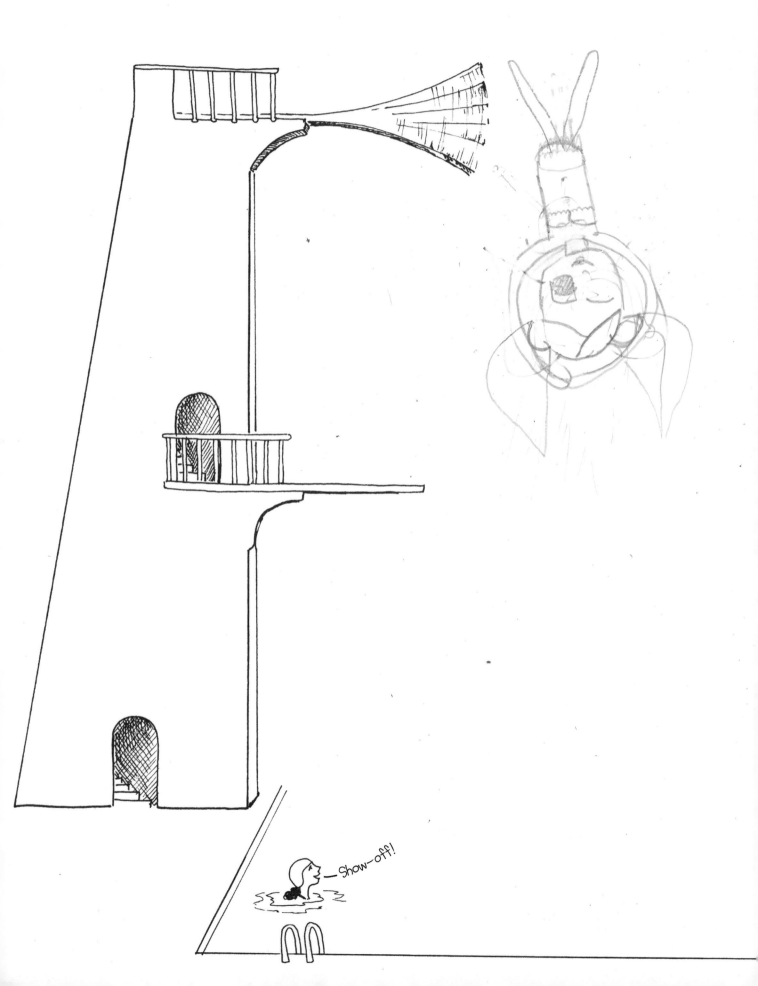

Build the world's biggest snowman.

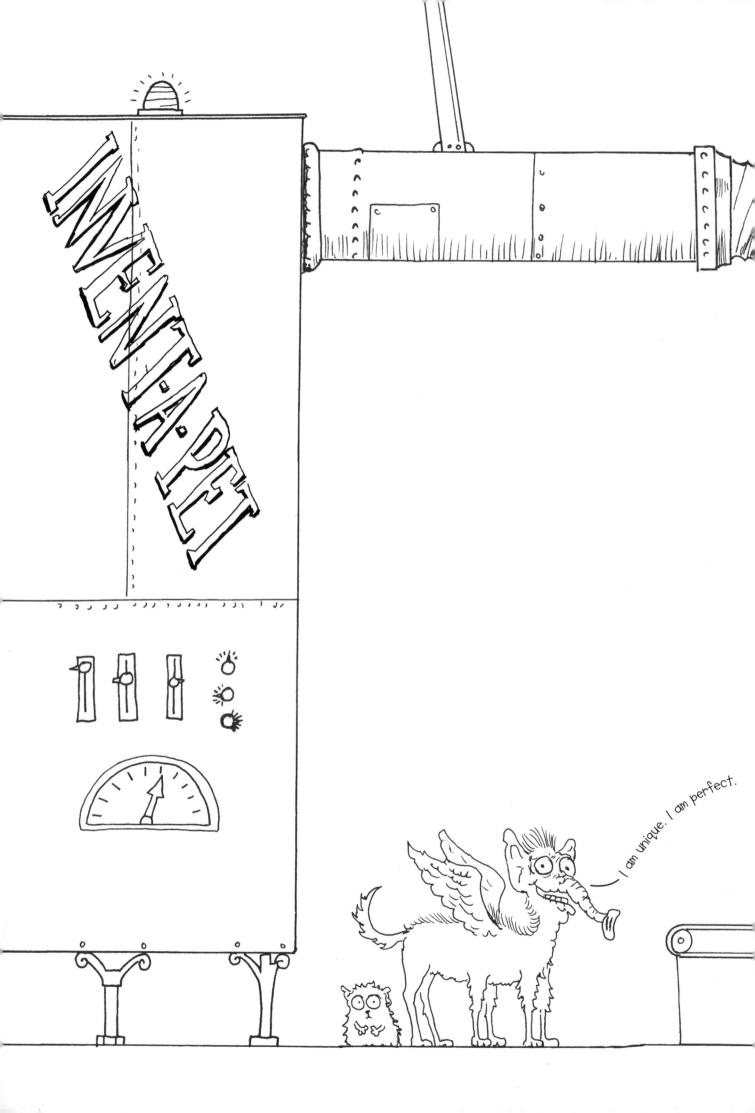

Design a completely new pet.

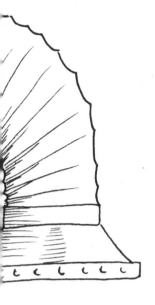

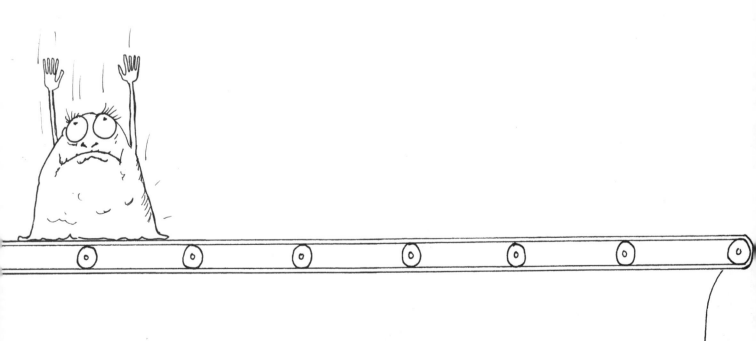

Who are they
following?

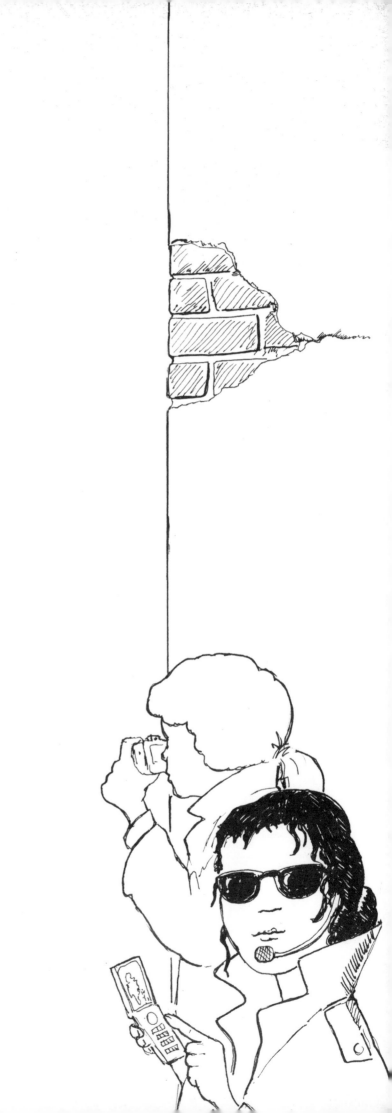

Who is sitting in the swingboats?

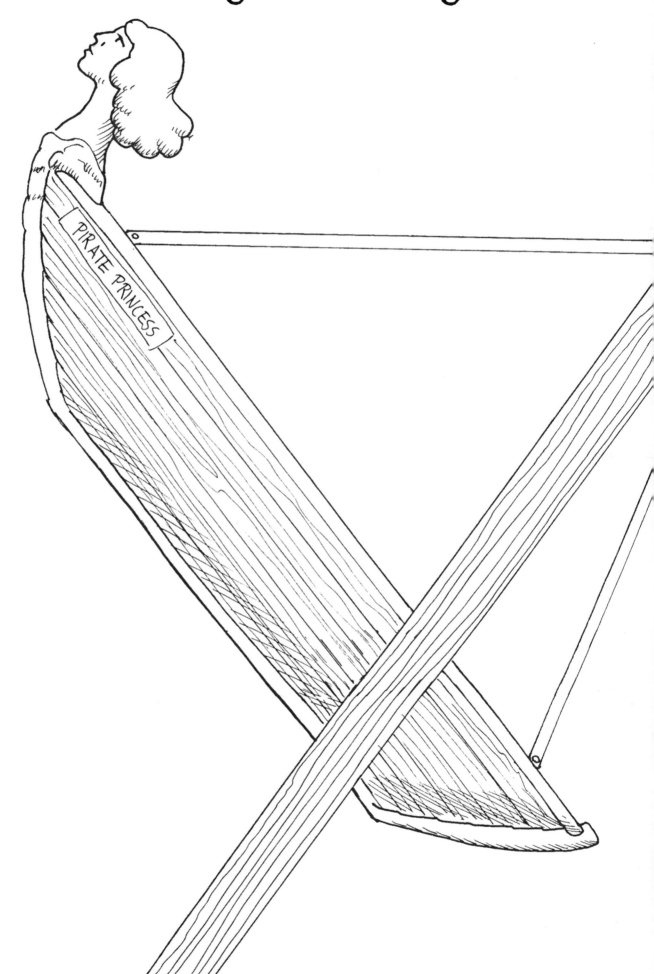

PIRATE PRINCESS

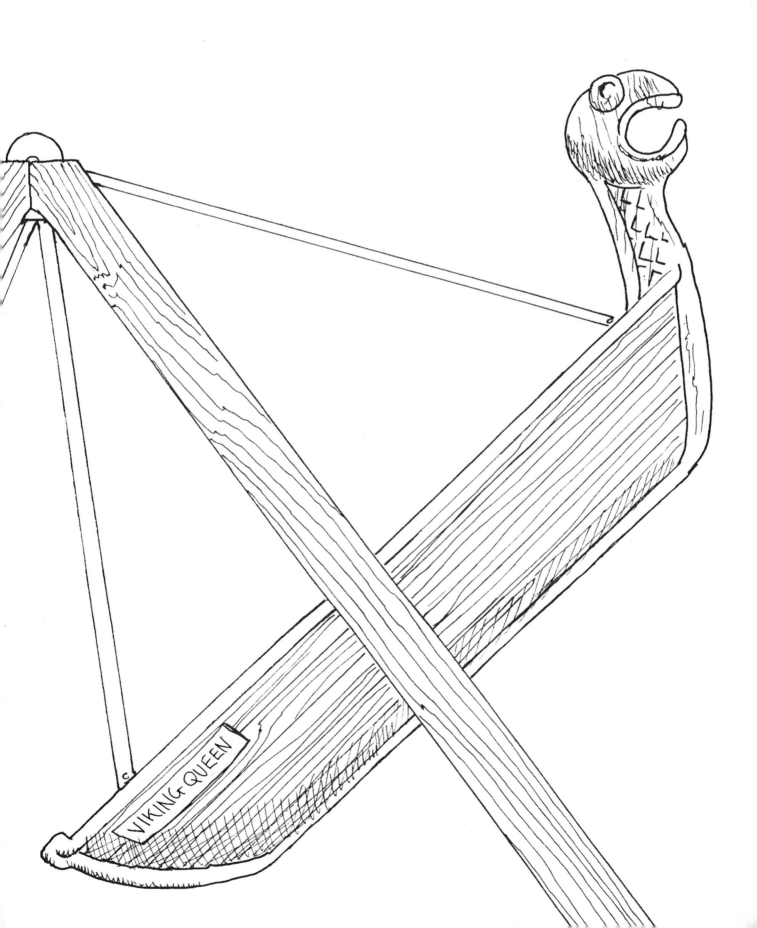

VIKING QUEEN

What has escaped from the zoo?

They went that way. Honest.

Who's kicking up the leaves?

Relax!

What is the princess sleeping on?

Who is crossing the rope bridge?

Fill the trees with woodland creatures.

Who is sitting around the campfire?

Fill the shelves with toys.

Put Cleopatra on her throne.

How will she get down?

Windsurfer girls.

Fill the candy jars . . .

... and the chocolate boxes.

Complete the street.

POSH FROCKS   JOKE SHOP

Who is coming to town with the circus?

Roll up. Roll up!

Decorate the beach hut.